POCKET
Guidebook
<u>TO</u> Divorce

JAN TYNAN-PARKER

Contents

First published in Australia in 2024 by Jan Tynan-Parker
jan@emerald88.com

 A catalogue record for this
work is available from the
National Library of Australia

ISBN: 978-0-6456665-9-5 (Paperback)
ISBN: 978-0-646-89914-5 (Ebook)

Print and ebook by Ingram Spark

Foreword

This Pocket Guidebook does not advocate divorce. I wrote it for people either thinking of or going through the process of divorce.

My intention was to write a guide that you could refer to often and feel reassured you'll be OK in the end. It is neither a review of marriage nor an academic account of steps to divorce. It is an oversight of what to expect and how to cope as your marriage moves to divorce. It draws on my own experiences and of those I interviewed for this book.

It is intended for everyone from all backgrounds and differing cultural, racial, and economic circumstances. It is not only for those with lots of money. Divorce more often happens to those with little or no money.

Over the course of two years, I conducted 150 confidential interviews throughout the world with people who have experienced divorce. Some more than once. I was privileged to hear their incredible life stories. Without choosing to sensationalise the details of their lives and personal experiences, this book will be sharing the recollections of how they felt and what they believe could've been managed better with hindsight.

Although each case is individual, there is a noticeable pattern of mistakes. My hope is to help you avoid repeating them or be aware of what they are.

The interviews were conducted with:

- divorced men and women, some of whom had married more than once
- children, who were keen to share their thoughts
- friends, family, hairdressers, psychics, and therapists as well as those who are part of vital support networks
- divorce lawyers in London United Kingdom, and Sydney Australia.

The interviewees who'd experienced divorce, reflected on the time when:

- they were triggered
- they were living in a dysfunctional, separated state of a family
- they came through the other side.

As a disclaimer, any reference to 'some people' or 'some children' is a reference to specific comments and insights from the recorded transcripts of those interviewed. It is not intended as a universal truth.

I've created this book in a convenient size, so you can carry it with you wherever you go. The cover is designed so you can read it in public without compromising your privacy.

I wish the best for everyone going through this difficult time and hope my book will help you navigate the emotional and practical minefield of divorce.

CHAPTER 1

Marriage to Divorce

Once upon a time everyone held the expectation of being married, with a belief that marriage was forever. To live happily ever after.

Marriage exists in all human societies, past and present. It was either a religious sacrament, a legally binding contract or a non-binding ritual between a man and a woman.

Marriage, viewed in simplistic universal terms, ensured the rights of partners, and in some cases, defined the rights of the children.

Consummating the marriage and fertility of the wife were major considerations. In medieval England, couples were permitted to marry on the porch of a church and live as a married couple for a year. This was to ensure the wife was able to bear children. If all went well, the marriage was finalised inside the church, a year to the day after the *porch wedding*[2].

Once there was no option to divorce in most cultures. To overcome this obstacle, women sometimes took matters into their own hands.

For example, in 17th Century Italy, an estimated 600 husbands were killed by their wives quietly and quickly, using *Aqua Tofana*[2], named after its creator, Giulia Tofana. Most likely made from a concoction of arsenic, lead, and belladonna, *Aqua Tofana* was a popular poison sold by Giulia Tofana for almost 20 years until she was brought to justice and executed[3].

Another widespread killing of husbands using poison was in early 20th Century Hungary. Zsuzsanna Fazekas, the ringleader of the *Angel Makers of Nagyrév*[4], first killed her husband with arsenic, before peddling her poison to the many other wives so aggrieved. By the time Fazekas was caught, tried and executed, up to 300 men were killed. The positive outcome in her case, however, was a paradigm shift in the minds of the husbands in Hungary at this time. Their behaviour showed great improvement following the evidence of death by poisoning with the exhumation of many of the murdered husbands.

Even when divorce laws were first introduced, only very wealthy men were able to entertain the idea as the costs were prohibitive. Divorce laws evolved, and costs reduced, though it was still men who exclusively filed for divorce. They had the money and power. This is no longer the case. Everyone can file for divorce without issue, in most countries. Even in those with strict religious restrictions.

In some jurisdictions today, marriage and divorce includes LGBTQI+ couples. These couples can also benefit from the protection of their rights.

Other jurisdictions today continue to defer to the customs and traditions of an arranged marriage. In these cases, the couple will have little or no say as to who their life partner will be. This may, in some instances, create additional pressures on a relationship.

Once people were expected to marry within the confines of their own borders. This is no longer the case in most countries.

Globalisation has created a negative as well as positive dimension to marriage. Despite being more commonplace, in many jurisdictions, cross-cultural, mixed-race, and inter-faith marriages experience different and specific issues throughout a marriage.

In addition to everything else couples must contend with today, the additional pressures and associated problems of living in a materialistic world, the burning desire to have everything all at once creates pressure. Aspirations such as money, real estate, jewellery, fancy cars, fame, spiritualism, wellness, inner peace, and on and on are desired without looking at how to obtain them. Marriage may not be the easy route.

This chapter looks at the experiences of the interviewees around

- deciding it's time to divorce
- how it feels when you decide
- timeframes between deciding and acting.

1.1

**STAND-OUT COMMENTS FROM
THOSE INTERVIEWED**

Before we get into detail, let's look at
a few comments made by those
interviewed that really stood out for me.

- Marriage doesn't always relate to love.
- Communication is the key. With bad
  communication, everything becomes bad.
- Truth, as opposed to love, is what counts.
- There is no way to predict the future person
  you marry.
- If you analyse those you've had prior
  relationships with, you'll protect yourself
  early.
- Marriage is a relationship, which is complex
  and deep. It creates boundaries.
- Romance itself is redefined with marriage.
- Some marriages are a reaction against
  the relationship their parents had: too
  co-dependent, too patriarchal, too toxic,
  strange belief systems, a way of life being the
  antithesis to what one partner wants.
- You will continue to vacillate until you wake
  up one day and know.
- You will decide it's over when it's over in your
  mind.

- When either person in a couple evolves and grows at a different rate or goes off in a different direction, divorce happens.
- Hairdressers will often know the story before you.
- Your world will change forever. It starts the moment you think of filing for divorce.
- There will be several relationships throughout the lifetime of a marriage: a beginning, a middle, and an end.
- Check yourself before you wreck yourself.

1.2

WHEN DO YOU KNOW?

Interviewees said that there will always be a trigger. These are some that were mentioned.

- Discrete infidelity.
- Flagrant flaunting of infidelity, indifference to your feelings.
- A partner packing up and leaving the marital home.
- A husband feeling emasculated by his wife.
- A wife feeling patronized and belittled by her husband.
- No more sex or intimacy.
- Dishonesty.

- Broken trust – a partner needs to always have your back.
- A partner who is jealous and controlling.
- A partner who is too focused on work and self-engrossed in personal interests and sports.
- Continuous nagging.
- Both become incompatible – different friends and lifestyle choices.
- Feeling alone or just wanting to be alone.
- A partner becoming immersed in the practices of a new fundamental religious faith, or political ideology.
- Years of emotional abuse and loneliness.
- A partner's family becoming too interfering in your life.
- A partner's prejudiced behaviour towards your children from a previous marriage.
- A partner coming out as LGBTQI+.
- A partner joining a cult, depleting joint finances. Might insist on living by strict oaths of the cult. For example, to remain celibate.
- Circumstantial change in the structure of the family. For example, one child may have special needs and require exceptional attention. The demands on one parent may be too great to sustain a marriage.
- Cultural differences affecting your family way of life.
- You've just had enough.

Some of the triggers that interviewees talked about were extreme:

- Domestic abuse – either physical, emotional, and/or financial, perpetrated by your partner. The abuser could be the wife.
- Drug addiction or alcoholism. This may not have been evident prior to marriage.
- Clinical narcissism. Warning signs can be evident prior to marriage.
- An extreme, untreated and/or undiagnosed psychiatric condition and/or psychosis. This may not have been evident or known on marrying.
- Attempted murder.
- Kidnapping or attempted kidnapping of your child/children.
- Sexual abuse of a child by either parent.
- Sexual abuse of a child by someone other than one of the parents.
- Death of a child.

1.3

FEELINGS ATTACHED TO DECIDING IT'S OVER

Here are some positive feelings mentioned by interviewees:

- relief and liberation
- courage and empowerment

- confidence, strength, and singular determination
- emotional control
- focus and survival mode.

Here are some negative feelings they mentioned:
- shock, terror and trauma
- anger and denial
- loneliness and sadness
- self-blame and inadequacy
- resentment
- victim mode
- a craving for affection
- no feelings at all

1.4

TIMEFRAMES BETWEEN DECIDING & ACTING

The most common timeframe to act on the decision to divorce was two to four years. The main reasons were:
- A need to overcome fear and proceed with confidence.
- It wasn't a priority for either party.
- One partner wanted to remarry.

- The grief for the loss of a child had to run its course.
- They needed the time to have therapy to be ready to proceed.

Very few people took immediate action to file for divorce. Those who filed for divorce immediately, did so because:

- They married young... realised it wasn't working.
- Their partner left the house to live with another.
- Their partner left with all the money and no third party involved.
- They or their partner wanted to remarry.
- Their life was in danger.

Some took a little longer (around six months) if:

- They had to wait for their partner to be away.
- They needed to recover from the shock of one partner leaving.
- They needed the time to research the issues of divorce and the process prior to filing.
- Their partner attempted to murder them, and they were in shock.

The balance of those interviewed waited ten years or more. The reasons given for this length of delay was:

- Working towards becoming financially independent.
- Waiting for their children to finish school. (The children interviewed said this is not a wise decision.)
- Fed up waiting for their partner to start the process.

For those who were older than 35 years of age and in their second marriage, the timeframe was five years or less to act and file. Subsequent marriages took even less than that. Both partners admitted the marriage was over without argument.

You will know when and why you decided that your marriage was or is over.

You may identify with one or many of the triggers in this chapter.

You may find you've experienced or will experience more emotions than you realise.

Act on your intuition. Be prepared.

CHAPTER 2

What you need to know

This list is a compilation of what both those interviewed advise as well as what the divorce lawyers have to say. The points made by the divorce lawyers may not be applicable to all jurisdictions.

It is important to note that a divorce lawyer is additionally referred to as a solicitor. Throughout this book I refer to both divorce lawyer and/or solicitor.

Once again, please note the disclaimer that these points have been taken from transcripts of those people interviewed. You need to research everything yourself in relation to filing for a divorce. Do not expect the law to work in the way you anticipate.

This chapter covers:

- General Information and documentation required
- What to include in your Initial Brief
- In relation to the children
- About the process
- In relation to the lawyer
- Choosing a lawyer
- Your choice of lawyer – some red flags
- In relation to finance
- Where to divorce
- Filing without legal representation
- What to expect from non-divorced people.

2.1

GENERAL INFORMATION & DOCUMENTATION REQUIRED

- Be mindful that it is not compulsory to use a divorce lawyer. Many successful divorces are filed by either one partner or jointly, without legal representation.

- Understand from the outset that your solicitor is not your therapist. A solicitor will cost a lot more than a qualified therapist.

- Determine what the solicitor does and what you need to do to build your case.

- Do not be surprised if everyone you thought you could count on lets you down.

- The best people to advise are those who've been through the process themselves.

- If divorce has been thrust upon you, accept the situation. Engage a divorce lawyer. File your application to the relevant court and serve as early as possible.

- If filing jointly be sure this is in your best interests.

- So many people interviewed argued about who will keep the family photographs. Make sure you have a copy of all negatives/digital files to eliminate this issue.

- Research as much as possible on the process. Demonstrate to your divorce lawyer you are ready to take on the process as per the outline below:

- Prepare ahead for the first meeting with any divorce lawyer or mediator.
  - Write an initial brief. This is a document, which serves as an introduction to the facts of the case. Send this to your solicitor for review prior to the first meeting. It must be an honest, well edited document, without emotion.

WHAT TO INCLUDE IN YOUR INITIAL BRIEF:

  - Your full name, nationalities, date of birth, current residential address, employment and contact details.
  - Your partner's full name, nationalities, date of birth, current residential address, employment and contact details.
  - Date and location of your marriage. A copy of your marriage certificate can be provided later.
  - The full names, nationalities and details of all children including any you are looking after as a stepparent. Provide individual dates of birth, current residential addresses, and details of all schools attended by each child, if applicable.
  - The names, breeds and details of all pets including those which may have joined the family after the marriage or come from a former marriage. Detail the date

they became part of the current family. Be ready to provide proof of ownership. It may become important in proving who is the master of the pet .

- A brief outline of your marriage and why you are filing for divorce. Outline the relationship between you and your partner from when you were married until when the marriage broke down. Provide the timeline and reasons of how and why the dynamics of the marriage changed.
- If currently living together or apart, include whether you are still having a sexual relationship. You may be required to provide additional affidavits from others who could confirm this.
- Detail all countries you lived together during the marriage.
- If infidelity forms part of the reasons for divorce, summarise the details. You may be required to prove this and include hard evidence at a later stage.
- If abuse of any nature is involved, between you and your partner, detail when the abuse started. Explain what this entailed. Any photographs or evidence can be provided later. You may need additional affidavits provided by witnesses and others.
- If abuse of the children is involved, either by your partner or anyone outside of the marriage, detail what this is and express

any concerns for the children's safety, if applicable. Detail any involvement of Government Child Protection Services and steps taken to ensure the safety of the children. Evidence and additional affidavits from others will be required.

- If a child has died detail the date and events surrounding the death.

- If you've had to cope with unreasonable demands due to caring for a child with special needs or a child with a serious illness, both instances requiring exceptional attention, provide the timeline and details of how this impacted your marriage.

- If your partner joined a cult and depleted joint finances, provide details. If no permission was given, this can be part of the financial settlement. Proof can be provided later.

- If you have any pre-nuptial agreements, include a summary of the details. A full copy of this will be required later.

- If you have a written agreement of separation and/or divorce terms between you and your partner, provide a summary. A full copy will be required later.

- Outline and summarise your expectation in relation to the custody of all children, including any visitation rights during the process. This includes pets if they are cared for as if they were children or are important for the support of the children. Be very clear about what you believe is in the best interests of the children and/or pets and why. If there are any details, you are not willing to compromise in relation to custody of the children and/or pets state these here.

- Summarise your expectation of the financial settlement you would hope to achieve.

- Summarise all other important elements of the divorce terms you are not prepared to compromise on.

- Conclude by stating your expectation of the overall outcome you hope to achieve from the divorce.

• Provide honest information in relation to all financial matters. You and your partner will need to do so in a timely manner. There are many ways to source this information. For example, a partner on a salary will have records of their annual income with bonuses. Do not lie.

• Prove legal ownership of what you will be declaring as your property. Although most people don't do this, it is important to provide receipts for all items you purchased and paid for yourself throughout the marriage. These may be items at any of the marital properties or stored offsite. These will not and cannot be included in the financial settlement.

- Provide evidence of everything that has been gifted to you throughout the marriage, particularly high-value items such as property, cars, artworks, antiques, jewellery, carpets and fine art objects. Gift cards, notes, e-mails, deeds and titles are documented evidence of ownership. These gifts cannot be included in the financial settlement.
- Provide proof of any infidelity. Collect the evidence. You may need to engage a private investigator.

2.2

IN RELATION TO THE CHILDREN

Parents create the storm... it is their storm.

It's irritating to children that parents think they don't know what's going on. They can predict situations and may know much more at any given time than you will credit them.

Your children's experience of this difficult time can be improved by your behaviour as parents:

- Let them know you are always there for them.
- Remind them that they have your unconditional love.
- Assure them it has nothing to do with them.
- Arrange for them to see a suitable therapist as they're navigating the process.
- Keep a family and home environment with a structured and consistent routine.
- Assure them that one spouse doesn't have a problem with the child loving the other parent.

At the end of the day, it's the continuous and ongoing support that children remember.

Throughout the process, children who have one loving person supporting them will be ok.

2.3

ABOUT THE PROCESS

- There are typically two parts to a divorce. Three parts if there are children. The children will always come first:
  - The divorce itself.
  - The financial claims. These tend to be the most contentious and take the longest time. They also generate the most heat.
  - The issue in relation to custody of the children, if applicable. One partner may weaponize the children.
- Divorce lawyers must find out if the relationship is really at an end:
  - In the right circumstances and with the couple having the determination to mend the marriage, counselling could help.
  - If a couple is determined to be divorced, counselling won't work.

- A client will go ahead if they're reasonably serious.
- Grounds for divorce tend to be gender specific:
  - Women typically are accused of adultery.
  - Men don't like to be accused of unreasonable behaviour. If the woman can use adultery or any other grounds much the better.
- In relation to custody of the children, you need a good parenting plan and good advice regarding the circumstances presented to best represent yourself. For example, one parent may work and live in a different location, which needs consideration.
- Consider the wording of all correspondence to legal offices of family courts in jurisdictions where this counts. It should expedite responses.
- Ask for the agenda for any court proceeding anywhere. Read all preparatory paperwork.
- Be smart. Prepare for the initial hearing as if it were the last.
- Don't be coerced by anyone. Stand your ground.

2.4

IN RELATION TO THE LAWYER

The most important relationship throughout the process is that between you and your lawyer, also referred to as a solicitor.

- You need a lawyer you can trust. They need to be fighting in your corner always.
- Your lawyer should want to resolve all issues well and as soon as possible.
- Divorce lawyers agree, as a rule, not to act to prolong the process to earn a higher fee. If quoting unreasonable and exorbitant fees they have no interest in representing you. Only some lawyers are out to stack up fees.
- Some law firms provide a booklet to assist clients in managing their expectations.

2.5

CHOOSING A LAWYER

- There is no need for the best lawyer. Choose one who will represent your best interests.

- A recommendation from a trusted friend could be the first avenue to explore. Additional research on this choice is still required.

- Check the performance record of any solicitor you're considering.

- Whether young or old, male, or female, you need to choose a solicitor you trust. One with your way of thinking.

- The gender and age of the solicitor may be important for you.

- If filing for divorce on your own, choose your solicitor with consideration. Do not use a recommendation made by your partner and/ or any of his friends or partners of his friends.

- If you need more than one team of lawyers (perhaps your case requires additional overseas representation), ensure you seek trusted assistance. You need the best teams suited to your needs in all jurisdictions. The teams need to collaborate professionally and in a timely manner.

- Use your intuition.

2.6

YOUR CHOICE OF LAWYER –
SOME RED FLAGS

Not all lawyers have your best interests at heart. Some are simply bad; others may convey inappropriate behaviours or attitudes.

This list is compiled using the experiences and hindsight of those interviewed.

- If you learn your solicitor is representing your partner in any other matters, it's a conflict of interest. Terminate and find another one.
- A dogmatic, pompous, aggressive, racist and/or sexist solicitor is not a good choice. Do not engage.
- A patronising solicitor, who made you feel inferior during the first meeting, needs no further engagement.
- A solicitor, too arrogant to read your initial brief sent prior to the first meeting should not be engaged.
- A solicitor who flirts overtly to the point of harassment needs to be terminated with immediate effect. Consider reporting the incident to the relevant authorities.
- A solicitor who is 100% confident of achieving

all outcomes is a red flag. Solicitors cannot guarantee success in what they will be fighting for. Do not engage.

- If the first meeting is very brief this raises a red flag. You may not be well represented. Do not engage.
- If you come out of the first meeting more confused, find another solicitor.
- A solicitor intent on focusing on the financial settlement, may act out of greed. Big red flag. Do not engage.
- If filing jointly and you're being ignored, with an obvious bias in favour of your partner, engage your own solicitor.

Some people just don't get on with their solicitor. That's ok, look elsewhere.

2.7

IN RELATION TO FINANCE

- In some jurisdictions there is no legal entitlement to a 50/50 split of assets. It may depend on your contribution during the marriage.
- Change your will prior to the divorce process being initiated. This is important.
- Appoint a suitable power of attorney prior to proceeding to divorce. This is vital in the event you become incapacitated or can no

longer make decisions for yourself during the process. If you've already appointed one, ensure they represent your best interests. Terminate and reappoint as soon as possible, if necessary.

- Splitting assets can sometimes involve both partners, with individual contributions from each party in some jurisdictions.
- In some jurisdictions, not all inherited wealth is included in the financial settlement.
- In some jurisdictions, a trust set up in a marriage can be varied by the courts.
- Ensure all trusts are set up to protect the assets for the children. This is for all jurisdictions.
- In relation to inheritance laws the spouse can contest proposed financial settlements in some jurisdictions.
- Stop paying the mortgage for properties you are disputing. You may want to place a caveat over one or more properties.
- You may need to freeze all family accounts.
- If possible, have ongoing control of joint finances.
- Be careful what you wish for. If you succeed in determining your partner is mentally unstable for your own gain, it may backfire. You could be legally obliged to pay for all ongoing treatment.

2.8

WHERE TO DIVORCE

- You may have the option to file for divorce in a jurisdiction more favourable to your outcome. Research prior to confirming where you choose to file.
- You should look at where you were married or reside, as the jurisdiction could be more favourable.

2.9

FILING WITHOUT LEGAL REPRESENTATION

- Be clear about your rights.
- Still do the research if you file without legal representation.
- You save money by filing independently.
- The time frame for the process can be reduced.

2.10

WHAT TO EXPECT FROM NON-DIVORCED PEOPLE

Here's one more area of advice that we touched on in all interviews:

- Sometimes people will congratulate you or say they're sorry, without knowing or understanding the circumstances underlying your divorce. They may be projecting what they'd want or perhaps they're being snide.

- If people ask for details about your divorce, you're not obliged to answer. Those who tend to be so curious are those insecure about their own marriage.

- In a social situation, blended families can create awkwardness with people from conventional marriages and families. Children's birthday parties, dinner parties and events with both parents attending the same function are some examples. Some people are confused and can act a bit strange towards you.

CHAPTER 3

The Process Begins

Many interviewed said the most difficult time of the divorce was when the process began. They said they had to be courageous.

The majority stressed the need to separate negative emotions prior to filing for divorce. They often didn't and with dire consequences. When you're distraught your judgement goes.

This chapter walks you through:

- your first meeting with your lawyer
- costs and fees
- helpful comments from lawyers.

3.1

FIRST MEETING WITH A DIVORCE LAWYER

- Be conscious of how you present yourself. Your attire, body language, and demeanour create a first impression.

- Presenting yourself as your true self is the best choice to make. Be confident.

- Come prepared with all documentation required and ensure your solicitor has received your initial brief. In most jurisdictions, there will be a need to record a lot of information during the first meeting. This will include financial background and any issues with the children.

- If you're not confident to attend the first meeting alone, ask a friend, family member or someone from your support networks to accompany you.

- Refrain from being emotional and/or aggressive.

- Ask for an estimated time frame for the whole process. This may not be possible depending on your case. Your initial brief will assist to determine what will be involved.

3.2

COST & FEES

- Communicate your expectation of service and fees to your solicitor.

- Ask for a cost estimate and additional cost expectations if the divorce proceedings are likely to continue longer than first advised. It's not always possible for the solicitor to estimate the final cost for the entire process. The cost in some cases can be significant

- Ensure you're provided with a schedule of fees included in any letter of engagement.

- Be clear as to how much you are able and willing to pay.

- Your lawyer should be able to tell you it won't be less than so many hours at a rate of how much. Your initial brief is important to assess the case.

- Some divorces can be covered by a pension or social security.

- It is not typical to be sent a bill after the first meeting in most jurisdictions.

- It is expected, in some jurisdictions, to pay an initial amount into a solicitor's trust account, prior to instructions being taken.

- The best outcome is to negotiate a fixed fee, or at least a reduced fee. If a fixed fee is agreed, you may be required to deposit the full and final amount into the solicitor's trust account prior to proceeding.

- Keep track of all charges. Legal fees can escalate with ongoing matters.
- If you're satisfied with the fee schedule, there is no need to negotiate. Some people don't mind what the cost is.

3.3

DIVORCE LAWYERS' COMMENTS

- In some jurisdictions, it may assist you to file first. You can then set the terms and timing.
- If cultural considerations are a significant part of your divorce, do not engage a lawyer without the ability, expertise and/or experience to represent such complexities.
- Do not believe threats made to you by your partner to pressure you not to divorce. They are not lawyers and don't know the law. They also can't profess to know what the outcome will be.
- Don't be coerced by the other party to agree to anything. Stand your ground.
- Divorce laws in all jurisdictions are constantly evolving and updating.
- If there's insufficient money for both parties, the standard of living will drop for both. More so for the husbands.

- As a general observation, there's never enough money.
- Dealing with overseas divorce is a very complex issue. Especially when children are involved. The Hague Convention will deal with cases for custody and maintenance in jurisdictions which are members of this body.

The better prepared you are the better the outcome.

CHAPTER 4

Staying the Course

The process is now underway. Be ready to manage all expectations, including anything thrown at you during the process.

Some people interviewed didn't manage to finish the process. They lost focus. Even after many years, one person remained in a stalemate without a resolution in sight.

Amongst those who had divorce thrust upon them, several tried to reconcile. Despite trying to hold on to what they thought could be saved, they couldn't.

A marriage between two cultures, races or different faiths and belief systems did exacerbate the process for some of those interviewed.

All interviewed agreed that divorce can get worse to an extent you could never imagine.

Staying the course is not always easy.

This chapter is a guide to keeping you on track. It will detail:

- what to expect
- what the lawyers say
- identifying and dealing with bad lawyers
- how to cope
- looking at available support networks.

4.1

WHAT TO EXPECT

The summary below is a compilation of what those interviewed did and felt throughout the process. It includes what they would've done in hindsight

- Your partner may go against the terms mutually agreed, either prior to filing, or at the beginning of the process. In this instance, if you filed on your own or jointly, without legal representation, you must engage immediate independent legal representation before proceeding further.

- You or your partner may contest the original jurisdiction of filing. This could be to expedite the process for both parties. It could also be because a different location could better serve the interests of the one contesting. They may feel they have too much to lose if they accept the original jurisdiction of filing. Especially if there is a suspicion that an original agreement regarding the financial settlement could be contested.

- In some cases, you can expect affidavits full of lies. Affidavits are written statements of alleged facts, sworn, and affirmed to be true and correct. They are filed in court before your hearing and may be required by you, your partner, or other people, if applicable. They are required to verify facts supporting your case or that of your partner.

- If you find an affidavit submitted by your partner or anyone else to be inaccurate, or untrue, don't panic. Do all you can to resolve all issues directly with whomever has filed the inaccurate and untrue affidavit. Stop any such matters going to court.

- Very few of your friends will agree to write the affidavit you need most.

- The outcome will not be determined by the party who feels they have been more aggrieved.

- Don't presume your partner is going to behave as you think.

- Arguments over possessions held jointly are common. Decide which possessions you really want. If you are planning to move out and remove items from the marital home, only take what is legally yours and can be verified as such. Provide receipts and/or cards, notes/e-mails or other digital communication, deeds, and titles.

- Your lifestyle may be used as evidence against you in some jurisdictions.

- Your partner's solicitor should stress to their client the need to make full disclosure in relation to all matters.

- Some husbands may use religion as a weapon.

- Some people suffer serious illness as a direct result of going through the process. Others suffer psychosomatic symptoms during the process. For example, they may lose the ability to speak or no longer be able to walk if triggered.
- Some people cannot focus on their work. They suffer financial loss as a result.
- Very few said the process was amicable.
- The hurt and devastation can be the same for the second or third divorce.
- Above all else, find out what other people have done when they divorced.

4.2

LAWYERS' NOTES:

These have been compiled using the notes from transcripts of the divorce lawyers interviewed. Despite not being relevant to all jurisdictions, they provide some insights.

- All couples going through a divorce need to be reminded that time is money. The highest cost of disputes and area of complaints is in relation to family law.
- At the end of the day, it should not be about how much the solicitors/barristers charge.

The benchmark of how good your solicitor is should be determined by the outcome.

- Compromise and settle all issues as quickly as possible to save both time and money. Arguments can be ongoing between lawyers and clients. Focusing on custodial matters and co-parenting is paramount.

- Solicitors don't want to be involved with the emotional elements.

- The divorce process in some jurisdictions tends to be much faster than in others. These jurisdictions may have a different view on cohabitation.

- There are very few straightforward divorces now. These would have historically been divorces between couples who married young or for a brief time. Most would not involve large sums of money and not necessarily include children. People marry older now.

- The process of divorce can be exacerbated between different cultures, races, religious faiths and belief systems.

- Husbands often try to carve a wedge between their wife and their advisors. Particularly if the wife's solicitor is assertive. This is to the detriment of the wife.

- Dealing with family court applications can be destabilising and take months.

- Even though it is difficult, children need to have it explained to them that things are being done to protect their best interests.

- Sometimes parents need to meet in relation to custodial sharing. This can create tension and animosity. It's difficult for the children to witness. For example, temporary orders in relation to child custody tend to become permanent, in some jurisdictions.

- Some jurisdictions may be restrictive in relation to custody of the children. This is where research matters.

- There are instances where divorce must deal with the kidnapping of children. Each jurisdiction will have its own systems under their law. Others follow the Hague Convention.

- In relation to custody of children or financial settlement your lawyer will not always know how long it will take to argue these elements of the process.

- Although women are strong, they tend to be more fearful when dealing with divorce. It is helpful for everyone to research the issues of divorce. Your lawyer will take your emotional wellbeing into consideration.

- In negotiations, many solicitors instruct their clients to rehearse prior to hearings. It's all part of the game.

- In relation to financial claims the law requires a vast amount of information, disclosure documentation and paperwork in all jurisdictions. The process of sourcing these documents is referred to as financial discovery.

- Choose some points you're willing to compromise on. Decide what is non-negotiable.

- A lawyer, in some jurisdictions, can get into trouble for not ensuring their client is honest in declaring all assets.

- Do not lie. The truth will be revealed.

- Keep a very close eye on the case. Never drop your guard.

- For those experiencing multiple divorces, each process will be different.

- Divorce lawyers differ in opinion in relation to mediation:

FOR MEDIATION:
- Some believe it can sort issues in relation to children.
- Some believe it is underused in matrimonial issues: both parties need to be amenable to this route.

AGAINST MEDIATION:
- By the time it is considered, the marriage is over.
- It doesn't work without the structure of many courts.

- As a rule, it isn't as precise in relation to financial matters. In some jurisdictions there is no full financial discovery required to make it effective.
- You don't' know who is lying to whom.
- There must be 100% complicity between both parties.

4.3

IDENTIFYING AND DEALING WITH BAD LAWYERS

- Too slow in responding. You are not a priority. Address the issue or terminate if ongoing.
- Not communicating important new matters to be dealt with urgently. Terminate.
- Not following your brief. Terminate.
- Confirming secret deals with your partner's lawyer and not informing you. Terminate.
- Taking too long to transfer funds from the Solicitor's Trust Account to you. Terminate immediately and report to the relevant authorities.

4.4

HOW TO COPE

- It is paramount to prioritise the children's best interests and focus on their needs. In all considerations.

- Focus on being mentally strong as opposed to feeling like a victim. Feel sorry for yourself post-divorce.

- Use the inner strength you were not aware you had.

- Recognise when your strength becomes your weakness.

- Always think before you speak. Words taken out of context can create hostile evidence.

- Tell your lawyers only what they need to know.

- Acknowledge what your intuition is telling you.

- Follow up appointments and matters requiring attention with your lawyer. Do not let them waste your time. Be proactive to keep the process moving forward. Try to have a timeline for each element.

- Consider your future survival and financial settlement. Take time to consider every element of correspondence with your lawyer. Do not respond as soon as you receive a communication.

- Choose when to be accommodating and when to do everything necessary to protect your own safety and interests and that of your children.
- Ensure you're represented in the court relevant to your circumstances. For example, some people may have their divorce assigned to the Family Court when it should be heard in the High Court.
- Find a renewed focus on working harder and smarter.
- End relationships with your partner's family if you're being singled out as the bad one by your partner misrepresenting the facts.
- Remain hopeful. Surround yourself with inspirational stories of others who may have suffered much worse than you.
- Be aspirational. Imagine your future self, post-divorce. Don't dwell on the past.
- Always try to respond with kindness. Be kind to yourself.
- Keep yourself busy. Time alone thinking is not good.
- Take care of your physical health.
- Take up activities such as sports, walking, meditation, singing, dancing, reading, writing a journal, cooking, painting, or sculpting to list a few.
- Have some fun and go out. Do so within reason. Be cautious with all new

relationships. Don't jump at the first person who comes along.

- Ignore people who ignore you. They are not worth knowing.
- Beware of learned helplessness.
- Even if you're in an awful place you need to get to the place where it's safe.

ADDITIONAL THINGS TO NOTE FOR A SPECIFIC GROUP OF PEOPLE

There are additional issues arising for those who are either high profile individuals or where large amounts of money are involved.

Below are some comments made by those interviewed from this specific group:

- You may have to presume you're being followed and/or bugged.
- Your partner could be recording conversations.
- It is recommended to use a burner phone for private calls.
- Don't confide in staff/house keepers. They could be under instructions and/or paid to spy on you by your partner. Some even may be sleeping with your partner.

FINAL NOTES ON HOW TO COPE

- Don't get mad. Get even.
- Make full use of your support networks.
- If you go through divorce more than once, you may need to find new support networks.
- Always act with dignity.

4.5

SUPPORT NETWORKS

Your support networks will be paramount in helping you cope and stay the course.

Depending on how you relate to your issues, you will receive comfort, care, and affection when you have trustworthy support. You will feel less alone as you stay the course.

You will find out who your true friends are.

Those who support you most may surprise you.

SUPPORT NETWORKS & STRATEGIES THAT WORK

- Family
- Friends
- Pets and animals
- Hairdressers
- Psychics
- Therapists
- Your doctor
- Trainers/teachers in all things
- Solitude
- All elements of the arts and music

SUPPORT NETWORKS & STRATEGIES THAT WON'T WORK

- Your children
- Your lawyer, if you've instructed one
- A doctor who is a friend of your partner and/or sees your partner as a patient
- Your staff/housekeepers, if applicable
- Friends who are envious of you
- Someone disingenuous in intent hoping to gain from you failing
- Someone from your joint group of friends, known to be more supportive of your partner
- People who don't know you

4.6

FINAL NOTES ON STAYING THE COURSE

- Expect things to change from day to day.
- It's good to talk about it.
- Choose whom you share things with wisely.
- A good and supporting person doesn't mind you pouring your heart out. It doesn't matter how emotional you are when you share with those who support you.
- There is no right or wrong way to communicate your heartache.
- It may not be good to talk about it all the time.
- Look for alternative ways to be supported, other than interaction with people. Some Interviewed felt supported by immersive experiences such as reading a book, attending plays, ballets, opera, musicals, concerts; performing their own music; creating their own art; spending time at museums and art galleries; or just staying home and binge-watching relatable movies and series on streaming platforms.
- Seek resolution to issues as you go through the process.
- Know that if you had no role model or a bad role model for a parent/parents, you may find the process of divorce triggering and more traumatic.

- Know that a parent or parents who have never been supportive will not be supportive during this time of need.
- Remember that it's more common for a woman to be discriminated against during the divorce process. Women are invited less to intimate dinner parties/social functions once the process begins. Men can be invited more often than before.
- Don't rise to the bait if your partner attacks your Achilles heel.
- Don't continue a relationship with a lover who wants to marry and have children while you're going through the process.
- Realise there will be a divorce amongst mutual friends.

The most important take away from the interviews for this chapter is the paramount consideration of the children. The failure to focus on this consideration is one of the most acknowledged mistakes of those interviewed.

The next chapter is dedicated to this topic.

Considering the Children

Children didn't ask to be born. They must be considered first.

Children are the centre of their own world and will often blame themselves for the divorce of their parents.

Although each divorce process is individual, there is a pattern of mistakes made in relation to the consideration of the children. Of those interviewed, their failure to focus on this was one of the most acknowledged mistakes with hindsight.

For children, the process of divorce is traumatic. It unsettles the core of their world.

The children interviewed were disturbed most by parents not knowing how to communicate effectively.

Never underestimate what children intuitively know and are aware of.

Too often, one or other of the parents use the children in divorce.

This chapter looks at:
- children and the process
- how children cope
- considering pets (now often considered as children and in many instances referred to as *fur babies*).

5.1

THE CHILDREN AND THE PROCESS

The children interviewed all experienced being part of their parents' divorce, some more than once. This is from their point of view. It is their truth.

- Children experience everything.
- Children are traumatised throughout the divorce process and should be considered at every stage.
- Consider all communication with children. Use tact, positivity, and a neutral tone.
- Communicate what is necessary and age appropriate.
- Deliver news with honesty and without drama.
- Children do not like secrets.
- Not everything should be shared with children.
- Children tend to agree with the need to divorce. Most ask themselves not if, but when and how.
- Children believe parents need to have clarity of sight.
- Children are aware of their parents' flaws.
- Do not rise to the bait in a conversation with children.

- During the confrontational stage, parents may not even know what they're saying to their children. They should be more mindful to deescalate the situation.

- Some children are of the opinion that once there's a certain vibe or feeling, there's no need to talk about it. That which is not said can be more informative.

- It's important to include the word "we" in discussions with children.

- Parents need to look after themselves to be able to look after their children during the divorce process and after.

- Stability is important for a child to cope with all that's going on in a divorce.

- Children ask parents to remember they have a life and activities outside of the divorce process. They prefer living as they did prior to the process starting.

- Children from mixed-race marriages believe the process is even more traumatic for them.

- Children would like both parents to honour the boundaries agreed for joint custody during the process. They asked their parents to consider timetables wisely.

- With any separation during the process, both parents should do all they can to maintain a close bond with all their children.

- Children even as young as five years old are aware of manipulation by parents. They are aware when parents bribe them with money and gifts to buy affection.

- Boarding school is not a good place for children to be during the divorce process. Children say boarding school makes things worse for several reasons:
  - It's a sure way to end up having serious issues.
  - It's not possible to be on your own. Solitude is an important coping mechanism for many children.
  - You are often singled out as being different because your family has a problem.
- Children behave badly for a reason.
- Some sons will take on the role of the father of the family.
- Some daughters will take on the role of the mother of the family.
- Children disapprove of either parent demonising the other when speaking about them in absentia.
- Children don't like it when lovers are brought back to the marital home.
- Children say it disturbs them when parents have too many lovers too often throughout the process. They said it affected them by not believing that good relationships are real.
- Children said they are not part of their parents' support network.

- Some children believe that parents should stop being so selfish.
- Children don't like being used as blackmail.
- Children will blame the other parent if one is having an affair.
- Children will eventually learn the truth.
- Children worry about both their parents. This can become a burden too heavy to bear.

5.2

HOW DO CHILDREN COPE?

- Children described going through a rainbow of emotions.
- Children said they try to secure affection from both parents. It's a lobbying game. They said they must examine the changing dynamics of the parents' relationship.
- Children find many ways to help them cope:
  - Listening to music – one child described it as shutting out the trauma like a blanket.
  - Making or viewing art – drawing, painting, going to museums.
  - Playing sports.
  - Spending quality time with the family, both immediate and extended.
  - Having fun at school.
  - Getting on with life – a life away from the drama.

- Trying to make things peaceful. Doing everything possible to diffuse confrontation.
- Maintaining consistent boundaries for everything and everyone.
- Letting go of their anger. They said anger only feeds on itself.
- Finding comfort in communication with siblings.
- Choosing to live as if they weren't part of the family.
- Looking for kindness and finding new friends.
- Sticking with and working through any personal problems created by the divorce process. Perhaps feeling shame or becoming introverted and withdrawn. Some children started smoking, experimenting with drugs or drinking.
- Not dealing with issues on their own.
- Finding comfort where they live – for example, some said living in an apartment was less isolating than when they lived in a large house.

It's very sad when the children have no relationship with either parent.

Eventually it all settles.

5.3

CONSIDERING THE PETS

Pets are now more important and inclusive in all aspects of the life within many families. They need to be considered. Pets also suffer from divorce.

Further to this, it is now common for many married couples choosing to have pets over children. They are treated as if they were their children.

The significance of pets in families today cannot be underestimated. In recent years, in some jurisdictions, they have been elevated from chattel status to equal that of children. In many jurisdictions, terms for divorces will now include custodial arrangements and rights for all pets, whatever they may be.

In my opinion, it will be interesting to see how divorce laws evolve to consider the recent elevation in the status of pets within the family unit.

Pets cannot be overlooked.

- Many pets can read emotions of the family.
- Pets can be and are aware of what's happening.
- Pets might be affected in similar ways as children.
- It is important, in some cases, to prove who the true master is. To claim you are the master of a pet, have your name on the microchip and/or ensure the vet has you on record as the owner. Keep receipts of vet invoices in your name.
- Be mindful that pets may not always wish to be moving from one partner's residence to another.
- Some pets may dislike your partner to the extent of acting out and behaving badly.
- Be mindful your partner may try to steal your pet to hurt you.
- In extreme cases some partners will go the extreme of killing a pet as a threat or warning.
- Use intuition to consider the pets always.

CHAPTER 6

The Finality

As the process nears the end and divorce is becoming a reality, it's good to imagine what you want when it's all over. Visualisation and ruminations of a *future you* can help to create hope for a better life to follow.

Then comes the moment...receiving the document stating you are now absolutely divorced. How will you feel? How did those I interviewed feel?

In the end, everyone knew there was going to be a life after divorce. However, prior to reaching that milestone, most recognised the need for time to recover and heal. Some didn't and married again. Before too long many had to go through the process of divorce all over again. Some did this more than once.

For those who didn't have a happy outcome, they wondered why they went through the process in the first place.

Most of those interviewed did let go, heal, and move on.

Nearly all felt it was worth it in the end. Many felt a great weight lifted post-divorce.

Here are the true feelings, thoughts, and actions of those interviewed.

This chapter covers:
- imagining the future
- how it feels when it's over
- recovery and healing
- the future you.

6.1

IMAGINING THE FUTURE

Despite the challenges ongoing throughout the process, most of those interviewed were looking forward to the end and the life after.

- Some made definitive plans and knew what they would do and how they'd do it.
- Some looked forward to a new life and happiness, which they hoped would be long term.
- Some imagined peace, space, and silence.
- Some imagined aspiring to be like a never-forgotten childhood hero, heroine or idol.
- Some realised the urgent need to create wealth post-divorce. They either knew how to do it or learnt what they needed as a matter of urgency.
- Many imagined living in a house or space of their own with nobody telling them what to do. Peace, space and silence.
- Nearly all imagined a new relationship and/or a new family in a future life.
- Some said they would never marry again. Many who said this did so. Some more than once.

- Some found it difficult to imagine making new friends and fitting in.
- Some said the future looked scary yet exciting.
- Some dreamt of a new life far from where their partner lived. Even on another continent.
- Many stayed positive and had hope.
- Some said they weren't looking forward to anything. They didn't know what lay ahead. They could only live in the moment.

All interviewed were just looking forward to the divorce being final. That was all that mattered to them.

6.2

HOW IT FEELS ONCE DIVORCE IS ABSOLUTELY FINAL

Some of those interviewed didn't know how to feel at first. Others had very strong opinions on how they felt and what they needed to do to move forward.

- Some said it was just a piece of paper.
- Most said the time frame was longer than expected.

- Some said it happened when it was meant to. A belief in things taking their own course.

- Some were shocked and traumatised by the ongoing court battles regarding the financial settlement.

- Some didn't receive any justice. They weren't protected by the laws in the jurisdiction of their divorce. They suffered from a deliberate prejudice of a corrupt legal system.

- Some moved from where they lived. Either by choice or because their life would be endangered if they'd have stayed.

- Some said both partners were equally happy. Their relationship improved. They felt free, enlightened, and relieved.

- Some said emotional blocks and stress ended.

- Several suffered health issues because of the process.

- Some felt flat and isolated.

- Some said it was matter of fact with a change of life to follow.

- Some were underwhelmed.

- Some said their confidence and self-esteem had been beaten to a pulp.

- Some said they felt ashamed. They had been brought up to believe marriage was forever.

- Some felt strange; as if part of them had gone. It had destroyed a fundamental sense of themselves.

- Some felt guilty because their parents had an unhappy marriage and stuck it out.
- Some blamed their parents for manipulating them into marrying in the first place.
- Many equated it to bereavement. They started grieving the death of the marriage.
- Some felt guilty in relation to the children having a life left behind. A former life and family that no longer existed.
- Many said their children were angry. Some said their children started acting out once the divorce was final.
- Some said the children took sides with one or the other parent.
- Some noticed their ex treated their new partner the same way they did them.
- Some noticed the second wives did not want the children from a previous marriage to have their original standard of living.
- Some felt daunted being single once again.
- Many said mutual friends were not keen to invite one or the other partner over. New friends had to be found.
- Some women said their female friends were jealous of them achieving independence.
- Some said they felt people were happy when one partner had lost their previous level of income. They felt it served them right.
- High net worth couples with high-profile

divorces said they couldn't trust anyone. They couldn't talk about it at all.

- Some people realised they had been unaware they were a victim their entire marriage. Their married life wasn't real.
- Only a few said the outcome was fair to both parties. In these instances, both focused on the best interests of the children.
- Many were happy they were able to focus again on their business and careers.
- Some said divorce was still better than giving up everything.

6.3

RECOVERY & HEALING

Feelings are very raw and specific once the divorce is final. Anger and hurt are the foremost emotions to deal with post-divorce.

Anger is an important and healthy emotion, not to be ignored. Managing anger correctly means you will get over it. You're going to be OK.

Forgiveness is also part of the process of recovery and healing. This includes forgiving yourself and your partner.

Sharing some of what those interviewed did to heal and let go will provide insight for what you can do.

Many started some form of counseling or therapy.

Therapies and therapists are varied; a psychiatrist, a psychologist, a social worker, a masseur, a personal trainer, a yogi, a spiritual healer, a psychic, a religious counsellor, among others.

Many of those interviewed explored additional and/or alternative avenues:

- Some serious soul searching. Therapist – no therapist.

- Reviewing their marriage with honesty and awareness of mistakes made.

- Reviewing how their partner behaved, noting red flags in the relationship. Despite promising themselves to take note before committing to future new relationships however, some didn't remember the notes taken. Others were mindful not to go into a relationship the same as their marriage.

- Making a significant change in their personal appearance and behaviour: weight loss, cosmetic surgery, a new hair style/colour, an upgraded wardrobe, becoming health conscious, taking up sports, stopping smoking, drinking or taking drugs.

- Keeping on doing what they were doing to make them feel and look good. Some did this and changed their appearance for the better without consciously trying.

- Actively seeking new lovers/relationships, including having relationships which weren't serious. Just having fun.

- Going out with friends for a social outing and companionship.

- Acknowledging the need for time alone. It is ok to be single and to acknowledge the need to heal.

- Carving out time to focus anew on their business or career.

- Making money and ensuring to give back in some way.

- Upgrading an existing residence or moving to a new one. Could even be relocating to a different and faraway country.

- Finding solace in surrounding themselves with their favourite and much-loved objects.

- Removing all photographs of their ex from around the house.

- Realising the need for a period apart. Not staying in touch with their ex. Not bothering about what they are doing post-divorce.

6.4

THE FUTURE YOU

Your divorce will not be what defines you.

The *future you* will be the person you've become after it's all done.

By letting go, not hanging on to old wounds, forgiving and starting with a clean slate, nearly all interviewed blossomed once they had time to focus on themselves. Their focus shifted to the more exciting years ahead.

- Some went back to pre-marriage careers, activities or hobbies, which they loved, and became even more successful the second time.
- Some no longer felt the need to hide behind their career.
- Some changed their career or profession.
- Some were able to work again without the stress of the divorce process.
- Many made good money after divorce.
- Some kept a low profile for a while.
- Some relocated to another country.

- Most wives changed their names. Only one person interviewed needed the security of being Mrs. Somebody.
- A few people joined a cult. In all instances, it didn't work out. One left after realising it was a scam. They lost a lot of money.
- Some made sure they used the support networks available to help make their new relationship work. They became aware of issues early and went to therapy if required. This way forward was successful.
- Many chose to listen to their intuition in the future.
- Some used hindsight to realise the importance of the family institution with their new families.
- Some said they had found intimacy and new relationships with their children post-divorce.
- Some panicked about the thought of starting a new relationship. They found it daunting to learn how to date during a different time in a different world.
- For many, understanding the romantic tools of today, such as navigating love and dating on the internet, were unfamiliar and tricky.
- Some became overwhelmed when they fell in love for a second time. Many didn't feel the need to remarry.

6.5
FINAL NOTES

Although you're now divorced and life has already changed, a full recovery may take years.

Whatever you do and however you become your *future you*, you need to congratulate yourself for coming this far. You have completed the full divorce process.

All those interviewed were happy they stayed the course and obtained the divorce they wanted.

Some threw a party, some underwent cosmetic surgery, some went on a long vacation, and some enjoyed time out alone.

Without exception, they all felt relieved they survived.

CHAPTER 7

Children Post-Divorce

It is important to share what children had to say about how they felt after the divorce was finalised:

- Some children continued to blame themselves for what had happened, and the outcome at the end of the process.
- Some were stressed and anxious about the future post-divorce.
- Some were confused about their new role with each parent.
- Some thought they could've dealt with the situation better than their parents.

Each child will have a different experience. Here are the thoughts of the children interviewed:

- Many children thought it was going to be easier than it was.

- Most of the process, in their opinion, was out of their control. They had to accept whatever cards were dealt. They had no authority and there was nothing they could do. It was all in the hands of the adults. They felt the adults could've asked the children what they wanted out of the divorce.

- Some were accepting of the way that it happened. It was something necessary and required.

- They speak of the commonality of divorce amongst themselves.

- They are more resilient than parents give them credit for.

- Many didn't think it would change things as much as it did.

- Many said the whole process was a very negative experience.

- Many said that a decision to divorce earlier would've been better in the long run. This is despite having to face living in a worse situation at the time. They believed it was better to get it over with. Waiting for them to complete schooling is not a clever choice in the minds of most children concerned.

- Many believed their parents should've communicated faster and better with their solicitors in finalising a fairer outcome for their custodial obligations and co-parenting.

- Many believe in a time of separation between

their parents' post-divorce.

- Post-divorce, they prefer parents to wait and only introduce new partners once it's a serious relationship. They said they don't like being exposed to a constant stream of new people.

- Many agreed it was difficult to witness frequent relationship break-ups, accompanied by the repeated hurt these caused their parents. They said this re-triggered their trauma of the divorce process.

- They liked it if the parents prioritised them over a lover.

- In some cases, trauma didn't end with the divorce. These children had been suffering either physical, sexual, emotional and/or financial abuse by one parent throughout the time their parents were married. This continued in the same manner after the divorce. Divorce for these children was viewed as pointless. It made no positive difference to their life.

- Some said they had a need to let go of the memories.

- For many, it helped to find new friends.

- Some said being part of other people's families helped with the healing process. Seeing families that are kind and loving gave them hope for the future.

- Some realised a need to look after themselves post-divorce. They were no longer prepared to place their life on hold for the sake of their parents.

- Some viewed themselves as evolving separately post-divorce. They still viewed themselves as having a family nucleus, albeit a different one.

- Some living within a new family situation, and still having to maintain relationships with a former family, found it best to speak about the present and not bring up the past.

- Some said that anything was better than the way it was before the divorce. This was despite not understanding or knowing if anything positive was achieved for their parents. For some parents, the divorce outcome left them still as unhappy as when they were married. In some cases, worse off.

- One teenager stressed that even if they tried to hand pick the worst wife or husband in the world, they could never replicate the messed-up life experience of their parents.

- Most agreed that although the divorce may not have been perfect, they had closure in relation to the daily drama of being part of a broken family. They were given the opportunity to live in a better family situation than before.

CHAPTER 8

Conclusion

Just as there is no one recipe for a successful marriage, neither should anyone conclude or generalise about divorce. It can be amicable or like a sinking ship – when it goes down there is the propensity to suck everything down with it.

Divorce in many cases can be related to money and control. It may not be about money per se. In many instances it is used as an operative, representing anger. It is the transfer of emotion, anger, into a physical object, which is money. In turn, children are used for retribution. It is power expressed through the control of money. A physical way to hurt somebody.

People who aren't divorced don't

understand that you and your partner will have been living in an intolerable situation, sometimes for years. You should be respected for your courage to act. There are many couples in every country choosing to live unhappily forever rather than go through a divorce.

Divorce isn't an easy choice. Life as you know it will be changed forever. Despite this truth, there will always be couples divorcing and families broken. Disguising divorce by using a different term, such as conscious uncoupling, decoupling, a time out of the marriage, an agreed separation, will not prevent the permanent destruction of the family unit as it was.

Divorce is and will always remain the most significant trauma for all concerned.

Their real-life experiences shared by those interviewed and reflected in this book are honest and heartfelt. This concluding chapter will recap the most important elements.

With the adult interviewees, we were taken from their first triggers, to starting the process, to staying the course, to coming through the other side. They all concluded that with the knowledge they'd gained using hindsight, given the chance to go through the same process again, the outcomes might've been better.

With the child interviewees, we learnt how they were affected, what they thought about their parents' behavior, and what helped them to cope. All children interviewed agreed that divorce is something no child should ever have to go through.

All lawyers' notes and comments throughout this book, including those at the end of this conclusion, are a summary of the interviews with renowned divorce lawyers from the United Kingdom and Australia. Some comments and notes do not relate universally to all jurisdictions and some comments are their individual opinions. Their insights are to empower and assist you further as you navigate your own unique process of divorce. Their final comments were unanimous:

- the better prepared you are, the better the outcome for everyone.
- even though it's difficult, divorce is not the end of the world.

8.1

A RECAP OF THINGS THAT HELPED

- Realising the marriage is over.
- Confiding in people you can trust and know well.
- Removing the anger and emotion before proceeding with the legal process of divorcing.
- Choosing a qualified and strong legal team you trust.
- Writing and sending a detailed initial brief prior to the first meeting with a solicitor.
- Being conscious of only speaking when necessary.
- Having faith that however bad the worst partner is, the truth will rise to the surface.
- Using strong and trusted support networks.
- Focusing on work.
- Taking care of your health and mental wellbeing.
- Keeping yourself busy. Too much time alone is not good.
- Only taking what is legally yours from the marital home.
- Remaining dignified and remembering your ex is also a parent of your children.

8.2

LOOKING BACK WITH HINDSIGHT

As outlined in the Foreword, each divorce is individual, yet there is a noticeable pattern of mistakes made. Throughout each chapter those interviewed shared what they believe could've been managed better with hindsight. Below is a summary of what they thought important to have known earlier.

- Some said never marry
- Always have a contract to define the parameters for any serious relationship. This can include all elements of a relationship.
- Try to maintain a sexual relationship and intimacy with your partner before the trigger to divorce occurs.
- Stick with any problems in your marriage. Start therapy or try to work through it together.
- Rely on those who've experienced the process. They can help you know what to expect at every stage of the process.
- Listen to your intuition.
- Change your will as soon as you think of divorcing.

- Appoint a power of attorney prior to starting the divorce process. Make sure this person will represent your best interests.
- Research as much as possible on the divorce process. Information is always there; you will only listen when you're ready.
- Do not expect the law to work in the way you expect.
- Know that your lawyer is not your therapist. A lot of clients regard their lawyers as emotional props or therapists. They are neither of these things. Apart from being the most expensive option for therapy, they don't want to be involved with the emotional elements of your divorce.
- Ensure all financials are in order before you proceed.
- Never share bank accounts and make your partner pay for as much as possible.
- Keep all receipts/invoices, deeds, titles, cards, e-mails, and notes for gifts. Gifts can be of a general nature and include properties, cars, jewellery, artworks and antiques.
- Be as pro-active as possible. Don't delay initiating the process.
- No need for the best lawyer. Find one who will represent your best interests.
- Tell your lawyers only what they need to know.

- Do not respond to your lawyer as soon as you receive a communication. Take time to consider.

- Words taken out of context can create hostile evidence.

- Learn how to identify and deal with bad lawyers.

- Appoint a new divorce lawyer as soon as possible if necessary.

8.3

CONSIDERING THE CHILDREN

- Parents need to let children know it's not their fault.

- Communicate honestly and without drama.

- Don't demonise your partner when speaking with your children.

- Let children have their own life and activities. It is not their storm.

- Don't have your children in boarding school while going through the process.

- Children are comforted if you facilitate a consistent home environment with a structured routine. Some children find living in an apartment less isolating than in a large house.

- Children need to be told they have your unconditional love.

8.4

LAWYERS' NOTES

Please note the following comments and opinions of the divorce lawyers interviewed.

- Stop marriages or update the contract for marriage with a more realistic account of cohabitation today.
- Most of the population don't obey marriage law in many jurisdictions anyway.
- Divorce lawyers advocate counselling prior to marriage.
- Prior to couples having a baby, they should take parenting classes.
- If you are married and have children, the real victims are the children in divorce.
- Very few divorces are amicable.
- One of the main triggers in divorce is communication. Bad or no communication means nothing will go well.
- Dynamics are shifting away from the historic divorce scenario: a couple who married very young and/or have no children, These couples were more likely to divorce and divorce earlier.
- One party might be triggered by one specific event. This can leave them traumatised.

- The most difficult decision of all is the decision to separate. It's downhill from there, however there will be an end. At that end you will start recovering. It's a cathartic process to come out the other side.

- Very few clients are focused. The best clients are those who come with all the information about the spouse they wish to divorce, the summary of all the financial disclosures and the background of the marriage and the grounds of divorce.

- There are many demanding clients. Despite the best and most appropriate advice given by their solicitor, these clients will not agree with the advice. Often to their detriment.

- In the opinion of one divorce lawyer, the worst people in divorce cases are pilots, psychiatrists, lawyers, and surgeons. This came from an observation over many years of representing divorce cases, that these people are control freaks by default. They hold peoples' lives in their power. It is easy for them to manipulate with ease.

- According to another divorce lawyer, CEOs prefer to resolve their divorce behind closed doors. Everyone is dealt with in an appropriate manner. There is always enough money to go around.

- Money helps when you're divorcing. Except when it comes to parents'/childrens' relationships.

- If you have enough money to survive the basic items of food and shelter you can breathe a bit during a divorce.
- Money is often used as a threat and a weapon. It's mean.
- In most divorces, men are resistant to pay what the woman expects.
- It's very hard to enforce child maintenance.
- Divorce with wealthy clients shouldn't be a war by default.
- Don't presume that whoever has the money won't want to hand it over.
- The true cost of a divorce is not realised. There's no happy outcome and everyone is going to be worse off:
  - assets are split.
  - your net worth will be halved or quartered.
  - it's often only good for the person wanting out of the marriage; for the one left behind it can be devastating, they're trying to take stock and catch up.
- The one deciding to leave can be ahead a year or two in terms of contemplating divorce:
  - structuring or planning how and when to do it
  - sorting out their banking and finances
  - deciding where they'll live and sometimes making those arrangements.

- deciding where the children are going to live.
- Everyone needs time to work out how to structure things.
- Many divorces are pre-planned.
- Don't rush the process. It will happen in its own time.
- For some, emotions are secondary to money.
- Men can suffer just as much as, or in some cases, more than women. Men also cry. This goes for any race, culture, religion, or location.
- It takes some time for clients to vent their anger and emotions.
- People coming out of divorce are often emotional and vulnerable. You are a target. Others can read this and take advantage of the situation. Bide your time post-divorce.
- Divorced men and women who look good, have plenty of money or are alone, elderly and wealthy can often be manipulated by predatory would-be new partners using good sex and charm. The cost of being duped can be staggering. In some instances, entire fortunes can be transferred to a predator or scheming new partner.

8.5

KEY POINTS TO REMEMBER

- You've lost what you've lost and won what you've won.

- If you brag about your wins your partner could claim more.

- Let it go. All relationships have a beginning, middle and end.

- There is neither blame nor should there be guilt in divorce.

- Review your thoughts on marriage and what it means. Convention and the current contract of marriage dictates that in marriage you agree to the presumed status of either husband or wife. What does that mean to you? What does that mean for same sex marriages?

- Think before you remarry. Analyse your choices of partner if you've divorced more than once. Try not to repeat the cycle.

- You made the decision to marry, and then the decision to divorce: your love turned to hatred, then anger. With indifference you divorced. At the end there was nothing more.

- People will still want to know about you even though you're divorced.

- Many people lose sight of the fact there is life after divorce.

Afterword

All the men, women, children, and divorce lawyers interviewed agree that a Pocket Guidebook to Divorce will be useful. They said they wished they had had it when going through their own process.

This book is our way of giving back. I am confident that with the reflections and advice from those interviewed, along with my own experience, your divorce process will be:

- less painful
- less daunting
- less drawn out
- less costly.

I hope this book helps you navigate your divorce with confidence.

ENDNOTES

1 Marriage
   www.britannica.com/topic/marriage

2 Porch Marriages
   www.rootschat.com/forum/index.
   php?topic=835584.msg7007256#msg7007256

3 Aqua Tofana
   www.allthatsinteresting.com/aqua-tofana

4 Angel Makers of Nagyrév
   www.allthatsinteresting.com/angel-makers-
   of-nagyrev

Milton Keynes UK
Ingram Content Group UK Ltd.
UKHW051604010924
447663UK00027B/221

9 780645 666595